Grammaropolis PRESENTS

WONDERFUL WORDS
FOR THIRD GRADE

VOCABULARY AND WRITING WORKBOOK

BY ORDER OF

The Mayor of Grammaropolis

Written by Christopher Knight
Interior Design by Christopher Knight
Cover Design by Mckee Frazior
Grammaropolis Character Design by Powerhouse Animation & Mckee Frazior

ISBN: 9781644420539
Copyright © 2021 by Grammaropolis LLC
All rights reserved.
Published by Six Foot Press
Printed in the U.S.A.

Grammaropolis.com
SixFootPress.com

Grammaropolis
PRESENTS

WONDERFUL WORDS
FOR THIRD GRADE

VOCABULARY AND WRITING WORKBOOK

GRAMMAROPOLIS BOOKS

HOUSTON

FROM THE DESK OF THE MAYOR

Greetings, fellow wordsmith!

Thank you so much for using this workbook. I hope you have fun learning some new vocabulary words!

As you know, many words can act as multiple parts of speech; it all depends on how they're used in the sentence. For the sake of clarity and simplicity (and because we didn't have enough space on the page!), the definitions in this workbook include only one part of speech for each word.

It's great to know a lot of vocabulary words, but the real reason we expand our vocabulary is so that we can communicate more effectively. That's why I've added a writing exercise, with optional prompts, at the end of each section.

Thanks again for visiting Grammaropolis. I hope you enjoy your stay!

—The Mayor

TABLE OF CONTENTS

HOW TO USE THE VOCABULARY PAGES

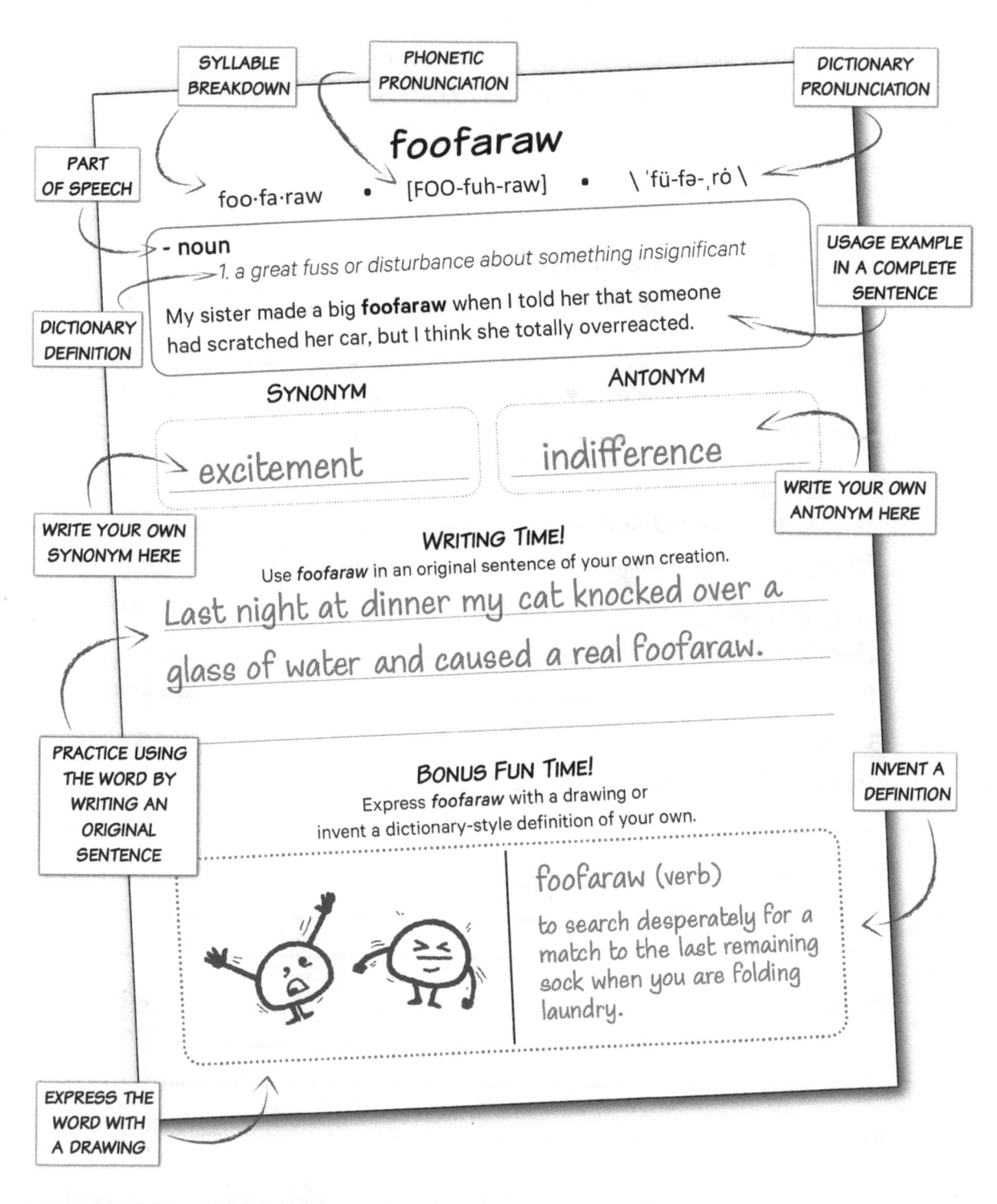

SYLLABLE BREAKDOWN

PHONETIC PRONUNCIATION

DICTIONARY PRONUNCIATION

PART OF SPEECH

foofaraw

foo·fa·raw • [FOO-fuh-raw] • \ ˈfü-fə-ˌrȯ \

- noun

1. a great fuss or disturbance about something insignificant

My sister made a big **foofaraw** when I told her that someone had scratched her car, but I think she totally overreacted.

USAGE EXAMPLE IN A COMPLETE SENTENCE

DICTIONARY DEFINITION

SYNONYM

ANTONYM

excitement

indifference

WRITE YOUR OWN SYNONYM HERE

WRITE YOUR OWN ANTONYM HERE

WRITING TIME!

Use *foofaraw* in an original sentence of your own creation.

Last night at dinner my cat knocked over a glass of water and caused a real foofaraw.

PRACTICE USING THE WORD BY WRITING AN ORIGINAL SENTENCE

BONUS FUN TIME!

Express *foofaraw* with a drawing or invent a dictionary-style definition of your own.

INVENT A DEFINITION

foofaraw (verb)

to search desperately for a match to the last remaining sock when you are folding laundry.

EXPRESS THE WORD WITH A DRAWING

Important Note: Synonyms and antonyms for nouns might be harder to come up with than they are for verbs and adjectives, but do your best!

THE PARTS OF SPEECH REVIEW

Every word acts as at least one of the eight parts of speech. In this workbook, you'll find nouns, verbs, and adjectives. Here are some things you need to remember about them!

NOUNS
A noun can name a person, place, thing, or idea.

Naming a person:
Jason is my very best **friend**.

Naming a place:
Becks Prime is my favorite **restaurant**.

Naming a thing:
That **ball** is my favorite **toy**.

Naming an idea:
Honesty and **loyalty** are my best **qualities**.

VERBS
An action verb expresses mental or physical action, and a linking verb expresses a state of being.

Expressing physical action:
Richard **jumped** across the river.

Expressing mental action:
Richard **considered** jumping across the river.

Expressing a state of being:
Richard **feels** bad. He **is** sorry for jumping across the river.

ADJECTIVES
*An adjective modifies a noun or a pronoun and tells **what kind, which one, how much,** or **how many.***

Modifying a noun:
The **quick brown** fox jumped over the **enormous red** fence at the **first** sign of trouble.

Modifying a pronoun:
They are **satisfied** with the answer, but I am still **curious**.

There are five other parts of speech you won't find in this workbook, but that doesn't mean they're not important!

ADVERBS
*An adverb modifies a verb, an adjective, or another adverb and tells **how, where, when,** or **to what extent.***

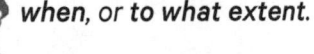

PRONOUNS
A pronoun takes the place of one or more nouns or pronouns.

PREPOSITIONS
A preposition shows a logical relationship or locates an object in time or space.

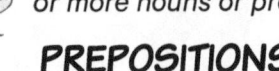

CONJUNCTIONS
A conjunction joins words or word groups.

INTERJECTIONS
An interjection expresses strong or mild emotion.

SECTION ONE: WORD PREVIEW

Welcome to your ten new favorite words!

When you encounter a new word, take a moment to consider what it might mean.

1. Think about the word and circle what part of speech you think it is. *(Many words can act as more than one part of speech, depending on how they're used in the sentence, **so only choose one part of speech below**.)*

2. Come up with a brief definition of the word in the part of speech you've chosen. It doesn't have to be the *correct* definition—just do your best.

persuade
Part of Speech: noun   verb   adjective

*Definition:*_____

_____

capture
Part of Speech: noun   verb   adjective

*Definition:*_____

_____

absorb
Part of Speech: noun   verb   adjective

*Definition:*_____

_____

gasp
Part of Speech: noun   verb   adjective

*Definition:*_____

_____

moisture
Part of Speech: noun   verb   adjective

*Definition:*_____

_____

responsible
Part of Speech: noun   verb   adjective

*Definition:*_____

_____

method
Part of Speech: noun   verb   adjective

*Definition:*_____

_____

ordeal
Part of Speech: noun   verb   adjective

*Definition:*_____

_____

disappointed
Part of Speech: noun   verb   adjective

*Definition:*_____

_____

process
Part of Speech: noun   verb   adjective

*Definition:*_____

_____

persuade

per·suade • [puhr-swAYd] • \ pər-ˈswād \

- verb

1. to cause (someone) to do something through reasoning or argument

Can I **persuade** you to build a fort with me out of couch cushions?

SYNONYM

ANTONYM

WRITING TIME!
Use *persuade* in an original sentence of your own creation.

BONUS FUN TIME!
Express *persuade* with a drawing, or
invent a dictionary-style definition of your own.

capture

cap·ture   •   [kAp-chuhr]   •   \ ˈkap-chər \

- verb

 1. to take, seize, or catch

Allison **captured** a funny little bug and put it in a jar.

SYNONYM

ANTONYM

WRITING TIME!
Use *capture* in an original sentence of your own creation.

BONUS FUN TIME!
Express *capture* with a drawing, or
invent a dictionary-style definition of your own.

absorb

ab·sorb   •   [uhb-sORb]   •   \ əb-ˈsȯrb \

- verb
1. *to take in or soak up by physical or chemical action);*
2. *to interest greatly*

I spilled my drink, but the paper towel **absorbed** all the liquid!

SYNONYM

ANTONYM

WRITING TIME!
Use *absorb* in an original sentence of your own creation.

BONUS FUN TIME!
Express *absorb* with a drawing, or
invent a dictionary-style definition of your own.

gasp

gasp   •   [gAsp]   •   \ ˈgasp \

- verb
1. *to inhale suddenly as an expression of shock or emotion;*
2. *to breathe laboriously with open mouth*

Willem **gasped** when he saw the size of the old cathedral.

SYNONYM

ANTONYM

WRITING TIME!
Use *gasp* in an original sentence of your own creation.

BONUS FUN TIME!
Express *gasp* with a drawing, or
invent a dictionary-style definition of your own.

moisture

mois·ture   •   [mOIs-chuhr]   •   \ ˈmȯis(h)chə(r) \

- noun

> *1. water or other liquid diffused in a small quantity as vapor, within a solid, or condensed on a surface*

The desk isn't completely dry; there's still a little **moisture** on it.

SYNONYM

ANTONYM

WRITING TIME!
Use *moisture* in an original sentence of your own creation.

BONUS FUN TIME!
Express *moisture* with a drawing, or
invent a dictionary-style definition of your own.

responsible

re·spon·si·ble • [ri-spAHn-suh-buhl] • \ ri-ˈspän(t)-sə-bəl \

- adjective
1. having an obligation to do something;
2. trustworthy in respect to financial or other matters

Juliet is **responsible** for making sure we are all prepared for the hike.

SYNONYM

ANTONYM

WRITING TIME!
Use *responsible* in an original sentence of your own creation.

BONUS FUN TIME!
Express *responsible* with a drawing, or
invent a dictionary-style definition of your own.

method

meth·od • [mEth-uhd] • \ ˈmethəd \

- noun
    1. a procedure or process;
    2. orderly arrangement, development, or classification

Marcus has his own **method** for building toy trucks.

SYNONYM

ANTONYM

WRITING TIME!
Use *method* in an original sentence of your own creation.

BONUS FUN TIME!
Express *method* with a drawing, or
invent a dictionary-style definition of your own.

ordeal

or·deal　　•　　[or-dEEl]　　•　　\ ôrˈdēl \

> **- noun**
>   *1. something that tests or is used to test character or endurance;*
>   *2. a painful or horrific experience, especially a protracted one*
>
> Spending the night outside in the rain was quite the **ordeal**.

SYNONYM

ANTONYM

WRITING TIME!
Use *ordeal* in an original sentence of your own creation.

_____

_____

_____

BONUS FUN TIME!
Express *ordeal* with a drawing, or
invent a dictionary-style definition of your own.

disappointed

dis·ap·point·ed • [dis-uh-pOIn-tuhd] • \ ˌdisəˈpoin(t)əd \

- adjective

    1. sad or displeased because someone or something has failed to fulfill one's hopes or expectations

Kevin is **disappointed** that he doesn't get to get ice cream today.

SYNONYM

ANTONYM

WRITING TIME!
Use *disappointed* in an original sentence of your own creation.

BONUS FUN TIME!
Express *disappointed* with a drawing, or
invent a dictionary-style definition of your own.

process

pro·cess • [prAH-ses] • \ ˈprä-ˌses \

- verb

1. to deal with (someone or something) using an official and established procedure

The clerk will **process** your request as soon as he is back from lunch.

SYNONYM

ANTONYM

WRITING TIME!

Use *process* in an original sentence of your own creation.

_____

_____

_____

BONUS FUN TIME!

Express *process* with a drawing, or
invent a dictionary-style definition of your own.

SECTION ONE: WORD REVIEW

Congratulations on learning ten amazing new words! Remember that the whole point of learning new vocabulary is actually to use it, so let's put your new vocabulary to use.

1. Review the words you've learned. Consider what ideas come to mind when you say the words. How about when you read the definitions?
2. Circle at least *two* of your favorites. You'll get to use these when you write your very own story!

persuade — verb
1. to cause (someone) to do something through reasoning or argument

capture — verb
1. to take, seize, or catch

absorb — verb
1. to take in or soak up by physical or chemical action);
2. to interest greatly

gasp — verb
1. to inhale suddenly as an expression of shock or emotion;
2. to breathe laboriously with open mouth

moisture — noun
1. water or other liquid diffused in a small quantity as vapor, within a solid, or condensed on a surface

responsible — adjective
1. having an obligation to do something;
2. trustworthy in respect to financial or other matters

method — noun
1. a procedure or process;
2. orderly arrangement, development, or classification

ordeal — noun
1. something that tests or is used to test character or endurance;
2. a painful or horrific experience, especially a protracted one

disappointed — adjective
1. sad or displeased because someone or something has failed to fulfill one's hopes or expectations

process — verb
1. to deal with (someone or something) using an official and established procedure

STORY ONE

1. List the words you've chosen:

_____

_____

2. Write a story that incorporates all of your chosen words. If you can't think of anything to write about, consider these suggestions:
   - **Write a story in which the main characters are you and your best friend.**
   - **Write a story that takes place at a birthday party.**

Title: _____

_____

_____

_____

_____

_____

_____

_____

Wonderful Words for Third Grade Vocabulary & Writing Workbook ©2021 Grammaropolis LLC

Caption: _____

_____

_____

_____

_____

_____

_____

_____

_____

Wonderful Words for Third Grade Vocabulary & Writing Workbook ©2021 Grammaropolis LLC

SECTION TWO: WORD PREVIEW
Welcome to your ten new favorite words!

When you encounter a new word, take a moment to consider what it might mean.

1. Think about the word and circle what part of speech you think it is.
   (*Many words can act as more than one part of speech, depending on how they're used in the sentence, **so only choose one part of speech below**.*)

2. Come up with a brief definition of the word in the part of speech you've chosen. It doesn't have to be the *correct* definition—just do your best.

active
Part of Speech: noun   verb   adjective

Definition:_____

_____

recognize
Part of Speech: noun   verb   adjective

Definition:_____

_____

average
Part of Speech: noun   verb   adjective

Definition:_____

_____

risk
Part of Speech: noun   verb   adjective

Definition:_____

_____

loyal
Part of Speech: noun   verb   adjective

Definition:_____

_____

swift
Part of Speech: noun   verb   adjective

Definition:_____

_____

remark
Part of Speech: noun   verb   adjective

Definition:_____

_____

vehicle
Part of Speech: noun   verb   adjective

Definition:_____

_____

certain
Part of Speech: noun   verb   adjective

Definition:_____

_____

passage
Part of Speech: noun   verb   adjective

Definition:_____

_____

active

ac·tive   •   [Ak-tiv]   •   \ ˈak-tiv \

- **adjective**
    1. characterized by action

My mom always tells me to get off the couch and be more **active**.

SYNONYM

ANTONYM

WRITING TIME!

Use *active* in an original sentence of your own creation.

BONUS FUN TIME!

Express *active* with a drawing, or
invent a dictionary-style definition of your own.

recognize

rec·og·nize   •   [rEk-ig-niez]   •   \ ˈre-kig-ˌnīz \

- verb
   1. to identify from a previous encounter;
   2. to admit the fact, truth, or validity of

I **recognize** that guy over there because I've met him before.

SYNONYM

ANTONYM

WRITING TIME!
Use *recognize* in an original sentence of your own creation.

_____

_____

_____

BONUS FUN TIME!
Express *recognize* with a drawing, or
invent a dictionary-style definition of your own.

average

av·er·age   •   [Av-rij]   •   \ ˈa-v(ə-)rij \

- adjective
  1. equaling an arithmetic mean;
  2. being roughly midway between extremes : usual or ordinary

My dog Coco is louder than most other dogs, but her size is **average**.

SYNONYM

ANTONYM

WRITING TIME!
Use *average* in an original sentence of your own creation.

BONUS FUN TIME!
Express *average* with a drawing, or
invent a dictionary-style definition of your own.

risk

risk　　•　　[rIsk]　　•　　\ ˈrisk \

- verb

1. to expose to hazard or danger

Justice is really careful with his money, but his sister **risks** hers by gambling all the time.

SYNONYM

ANTONYM

WRITING TIME!

Use *risk* in an original sentence of your own creation.

_____

_____

_____

BONUS FUN TIME!

Express *risk* with a drawing, or
invent a dictionary-style definition of your own.

loyal

loy·al • [IOY-uhl] • \ ˈlȯi(-ə)l \

- adjective

   1. *unswerving in allegiance;*
   2. *displaying or reflecting loyalty*

Neville will do anything for you because he is such a **loyal** friend.

SYNONYM

ANTONYM

WRITING TIME!
Use *loyal* in an original sentence of your own creation.

_____

_____

_____

BONUS FUN TIME!
Express *loyal* with a drawing, or
invent a dictionary-style definition of your own.

swift

swift   •   [swIft]   •   \ 'swift \

- adjective
   1. moving or capable of moving with great speed;
   2. taking place, done, or concluded within a very short time

Mr. Johns is a **swift** runner for an old guy.

SYNONYM

ANTONYM

WRITING TIME!
Use *swift* in an original sentence of your own creation.

_____

_____

_____

BONUS FUN TIME!
Express *swift* with a drawing, or
invent a dictionary-style definition of your own.

remark

re·mark   •   [ri-mAHRk]   •   \ ri-ˈmärk \

- noun
   1. a written or spoken comment;
   2. a mention of something deserving notice

Molly is always ready with a kind **remark** to make you feel better.

SYNONYM

ANTONYM

WRITING TIME!
Use *remark* in an original sentence of your own creation.

BONUS FUN TIME!
Express *remark* with a drawing, or
invent a dictionary-style definition of your own.

vehicle

ve·hi·cle   •   [vEE-uh-kuhl]   •   \ ˈvē-ə-kəl \

- noun
1. *a means of carrying or transporting something;*
2. *an agent of transmission*

When I can drive, my **vehicle** of choice will be a tow truck.

SYNONYM

ANTONYM

WRITING TIME!
Use *vehicle* in an original sentence of your own creation.

_____

_____

_____

BONUS FUN TIME!
Express *vehicle* with a drawing, or
invent a dictionary-style definition of your own.

certain

cer·tain   •   [sUHRt-n]   •   \ ˈsərtn \

- adjective
1. *known for sure : established beyond doubt.*
2. *of a specific but unspecified character, quantity, or degree*

Is it **certain** that we have homework over the weekend?

SYNONYM

ANTONYM

WRITING TIME!
Use *certain* in an original sentence of your own creation.

_____

_____

_____

BONUS FUN TIME!
Express *certain* with a drawing, or
invent a dictionary-style definition of your own.

passage

pas·sage • [pAs-ij] • \ ˈpa-sij \

- **noun**
    1. *the act or process of moving from one place to another;*
    2. *a narrow passageway, typically having walls on either side*

Passage on foot from California to Montana would take weeks.

SYNONYM

ANTONYM

WRITING TIME!
Use *passage* in an original sentence of your own creation.

BONUS FUN TIME!
Express *passage* with a drawing, or
invent a dictionary-style definition of your own.

SECTION TWO: WORD REVIEW

Congratulations on learning ten amazing new words! Remember that the whole point of learning new vocabulary is actually to use it, so let's put your new vocabulary to use.

1. Review the words you've learned. Consider what ideas come to mind when you say the words. How about when you read the definitions?
2. Circle at least *two* of your favorites. You'll get to use these when you write your very own story!

active — adjective
1. characterized by action

recognize — verb
1. to identify from a previous encounter;
2. to admit the fact, truth, or validity of

average — adjective
1. equaling an arithmetic mean;
2. being roughly midway between extremes : usual or ordinary

risk — verb
1. to expose to hazard or danger

loyal — adjective
1. unswerving in allegiance;
2. displaying or reflecting loyalty

swift — adjective
1. moving or capable of moving with great speed;
2. taking place, done, or concluded within a very short time

remark — noun
1. a written or spoken comment;
2. a mention of something deserving notice

vehicle — noun
1. a means of carrying or transporting something;
2. an agent of transmission

certain — adjective
1. known for sure : established beyond doubt.
2. of a specific but unspecified character, quantity, or degree

passage — noun
1. the act or process of moving from one place to another;
2. a narrow passageway, typically having walls on either side

STORY TWO

1. List the words you've chosen:

_____

2. Write a story that incorporates all of your chosen words. If you can't think of anything to write about, consider these suggestions:
   - Write a story that starts with your main character finding a suitcase containing a thousand dollars.
   - Write a story about the most disgusting thing you've ever eaten.

Title: _____

_____

_____

_____

_____

_____

_____

_____

Wonderful Words for Third Grade Vocabulary & Writing Workbook ©2021 Grammaropolis LLC

Caption: _____

_____

_____

_____

_____

_____

_____

_____

_____

_____

Wonderful Words for Third Grade Vocabulary & Writing Workbook ©2021 Grammaropolis LLC

SECTION THREE: WORD PREVIEW
Welcome to your ten new favorite words!

When you encounter a new word, take a moment to consider what it might mean.

1. Think about the word and circle what part of speech you think it is. *(Many words can act as more than one part of speech, depending on how they're used in the sentence, **so only choose one part of speech below**.)*

2. Come up with a brief definition of the word in the part of speech you've chosen. It doesn't have to be the *correct* definition—just do your best.

credit
Part of Speech: noun   verb   adjective

Definition:_____

_____

advice
Part of Speech: noun   verb   adjective

Definition:_____

_____

stumble
Part of Speech: noun   verb   adjective

Definition:_____

_____

furious
Part of Speech: noun   verb   adjective

Definition:_____

_____

continent
Part of Speech: noun   verb   adjective

Definition:_____

_____

event
Part of Speech: noun   verb   adjective

Definition:_____

_____

clever
Part of Speech: noun   verb   adjective

Definition:_____

_____

invitation
Part of Speech: noun   verb   adjective

Definition:_____

_____

respect
Part of Speech: noun   verb   adjective

Definition:_____

_____

woe
Part of Speech: noun   verb   adjective

Definition:_____

_____

credit

cred·it • [krEd-it] • \ 'kre-dit \

- noun
1. *the balance in a person's favor in an account;*
2. *a public acknowledgment of praise*

Sometimes my teacher forgets to give me **credit** for all of my work.

SYNONYM

ANTONYM

WRITING TIME!
Use *credit* in an original sentence of your own creation.

BONUS FUN TIME!
Express *credit* with a drawing, or
invent a dictionary-style definition of your own.

advice

ad·vice • [uhd-vIEs] • \ əd-ˈvīs \

- noun

1. recommendation regarding a decision or course of conduct

Do you have any **advice** for me about how to wrestle an alligator?

SYNONYM

ANTONYM

WRITING TIME!
Use *advice* in an original sentence of your own creation.

BONUS FUN TIME!
Express *advice* with a drawing, or
invent a dictionary-style definition of your own.

stumble

stum·ble   •   [stUHm-buhl]   •   \ ˈstəm-bəl \

- **verb**

    1. to lose one's footing so as to stagger or fall

Harvey **stumbled** on the uneven forest floor.

SYNONYM

ANTONYM

WRITING TIME!
Use *stumble* in an original sentence of your own creation.

BONUS FUN TIME!
Express *stumble* with a drawing, or
invent a dictionary-style definition of your own.

furious

fu·ri·ous   •   [fyUR-ee-uhs]   •   \ ˈfyu̇r-ē-əs \

- adjective

1. exhibiting or goaded by anger or passion

Saundra will be **furious** if anyone reads her journal.

SYNONYM

ANTONYM

WRITING TIME!

Use *furious* in an original sentence of your own creation.

BONUS FUN TIME!

Express *furious* with a drawing, or
invent a dictionary-style definition of your own.

continent

con·ti·nent • [kAHn-tuh-nuhnt] • \ ˈkän-tə-nənt \

- noun

1. any of the world's main continuous expanses of land

Antarctica happens to be Earth's southernmost **continent**.

SYNONYM

ANTONYM

WRITING TIME!
Use **continent** in an original sentence of your own creation.

BONUS FUN TIME!
Express **continent** with a drawing, or
invent a dictionary-style definition of your own.

event

e·vent • [i-vEnt] • \ ə'vent \

- noun

  1. something that happens : occurrence

Lee's birthday party was the biggest **event** of the summer.

SYNONYM

ANTONYM

WRITING TIME!

Use *event* in an original sentence of your own creation.

BONUS FUN TIME!

Express *event* with a drawing, or
invent a dictionary-style definition of your own.

clever

clev·er • [klEv-uhr] • \ ˈkle-vər \

- adjective
1. *having mental quickness, intelligence, or resourcefulness, often accompanied by craft or wit*

Crows are so **clever** that they can solve multi-step puzzles.

SYNONYM

ANTONYM

WRITING TIME!
Use *clever* in an original sentence of your own creation.

_____

_____

_____

BONUS FUN TIME!
Express *clever* with a drawing, or
invent a dictionary-style definition of your own.

invitation

in·vi·ta·tion • [in-vuh-tAY-shuhn] • \ ˌinvəˈtāshən \

- noun
1. *the act or documentation of inviting*
2. *the requesting of a person's company or participation*

Did you receive an **invitation** to the Chocolate Bar's grand opening?

SYNONYM

ANTONYM

WRITING TIME!
Use *invitation* in an original sentence of your own creation.

BONUS FUN TIME!
Express *invitation* with a drawing, or
invent a dictionary-style definition of your own.

respect

re·spect　　•　　[ri-spEkt]　　•　　\ ri-'spekt \

- verb

　1. to admire (someone or something) deeply, as a result of their abilities, qualities, or achievements

I **respect** my older brother because he knows a lot about Star Wars.

SYNONYM

ANTONYM

WRITING TIME!
Use *respect* in an original sentence of your own creation.

BONUS FUN TIME!
Express *respect* with a drawing, or
invent a dictionary-style definition of your own.

woe

woe   •   [wOH]   •   \ ˈwō \

- noun
    1. a miserable or sorrowful state;
    2. a condition of deep suffering from misfortune, affliction, or grief

Carlton was overcome by **woe** after his favorite team lost.

SYNONYM

ANTONYM

WRITING TIME!
Use *woe* in an original sentence of your own creation.

_____

_____

BONUS FUN TIME!
Express *woe* with a drawing, or
invent a dictionary-style definition of your own.

SECTION THREE: WORD REVIEW

Congratulations on learning ten amazing new words! Remember that the whole point of learning new vocabulary is actually to use it, so let's put your new vocabulary to use.

1. Review the words you've learned. Consider what ideas come to mind when you say the words. How about when you read the definitions?
2. Circle at least *two* of your favorites. You'll get to use these when you write your very own story!

credit —————— noun
1. *the balance in a person's favor in an account;*
2. *a public acknowledgment of praise*

advice —————— noun
1. *recommendation regarding a decision or course of conduct*

stumble —————— verb
1. *to lose one's footing so as to stagger or fall*

furious —————— adjective
1. *exhibiting or goaded by anger or passion*

continent —————— noun
1. *any of the world's main continuous expanses of land*

event —————— noun
1. *something that happens : occurrence*

clever —————— adjective
1. *having mental quickness, intelligence, or resourcefulness, often accompanied by craft or wit*

invitation —————— noun
1. *the act or documentation of inviting*
2. *the requesting of a person's company or participation*

respect —————— verb
1. *to admire (someone or something) deeply, as a result of their abilities, qualities, or achievements*

woe —————— noun
1. *a miserable or sorrowful state;*
2. *a condition of deep suffering from misfortune, affliction, or grief*

STORY THREE

1. List the words you've chosen:

_____

2. Write a story that incorporates all of your chosen words. If you can't think of anything to write about, consider these suggestions:
   - **Write a story about a time when you were in trouble.**
   - **Write a story that takes place in a cotton candy factory.**

Title: _____

_____

_____

_____

_____

_____

_____

_____

_____

Wonderful Words for Third Grade Vocabulary & Writing Workbook ©2021 Grammaropolis LLC

Caption: _____

_____

_____

_____

_____

_____

_____

_____

_____

_____

Wonderful Words for Third Grade Vocabulary & Writing Workbook ©2021 Grammaropolis LLC

SECTION FOUR: WORD PREVIEW
Welcome to your ten new favorite words!

When you encounter a new word, take a moment to consider what it might mean.
1. Think about the word and circle what part of speech you think it is.
*(Many words can act as more than one part of speech, depending on how they're used in the sentence, **so only choose one part of speech below.**)*
2. Come up with a brief definition of the word in the part of speech you've chosen. It doesn't have to be the *correct* definition—just do your best.

journey
Part of Speech: noun   verb   adjective

*Definition:*_____

_____

explore
Part of Speech: noun   verb   adjective

*Definition:*_____

_____

gradual
Part of Speech: noun   verb   adjective

*Definition:*_____

_____

elegant
Part of Speech: noun   verb   adjective

*Definition:*_____

_____

cause
Part of Speech: noun   verb   adjective

*Definition:*_____

_____

confess
Part of Speech: noun   verb   adjective

*Definition:*_____

_____

steer
Part of Speech: noun   verb   adjective

*Definition:*_____

_____

fierce
Part of Speech: noun   verb   adjective

*Definition:*_____

_____

arctic
Part of Speech: noun   verb   adjective

*Definition:*_____

_____

solution
Part of Speech: noun   verb   adjective

*Definition:*_____

_____

journey

jour·ney   •   [jUHR-nee]   •   \ ˈjər-nē \

- noun

1. *travel or passage from one place to another;*
2. *a long and often difficult process of personal development*

Becoming an Eagle Scout is a difficult **journey**, but it's worth it.

SYNONYM

_____

ANTONYM

_____

WRITING TIME!

Use *journey* in an original sentence of your own creation.

_____

_____

_____

BONUS FUN TIME!

Express *journey* with a drawing, or
invent a dictionary-style definition of your own.

explore

ex·plore   •   [ik-splOR]   •   \ ikˈsplō(ə)r \

- verb
1. to search through or into;
2. to make a first or preliminary study of

Let's go explore that **cave** and see what we find in there!

SYNONYM

ANTONYM

WRITING TIME!
Use *explore* in an original sentence of your own creation.

BONUS FUN TIME!
Express *explore* with a drawing, or
invent a dictionary-style definition of your own.

gradual

grad·u·al   •   [grA-juh-wuhl]   •   \ ˈgraj(ə)wəl \

- adjective

1. proceeding by steps or degrees : advancing step by step

Learning to snowboard is a **gradual** and sometimes painful process.

SYNONYM

ANTONYM

WRITING TIME!
Use *gradual* in an original sentence of your own creation.

BONUS FUN TIME!
Express *gradual* with a drawing, or
invent a dictionary-style definition of your own.

elegant

el·e·gant   •   [El-iguhnt]   •   \ ˈeləgənt \

- **adjective**
  1. tastefully correct and refined;
  2. of a high grade or quality

My aunt's house is so **elegant** that I don't want to touch anything.

SYNONYM

ANTONYM

WRITING TIME!
Use *elegant* in an original sentence of your own creation.

BONUS FUN TIME!
Express *elegant* with a drawing, or
invent a dictionary-style definition of your own.

cause

cause   •   [kAWz]   •   \ ˈkȯz \

- noun

1. a person, thing, fact, or condition that brings about an effect

Your whining is the **cause** of everyone's frustration!

SYNONYM

ANTONYM

WRITING TIME!

Use *cause* in an original sentence of your own creation.

BONUS FUN TIME!

Express *cause* with a drawing, or
invent a dictionary-style definition of your own.

confess

con·fess • [kuhn-fEs] • \ kən-ˈfes \

- verb
   1. to admit as true;
   2. to acknowledge, especially after a previous denial

I must **confess** that I'm the one who ate the last donut.

SYNONYM

ANTONYM

WRITING TIME!
Use *confess* in an original sentence of your own creation.

_____

_____

_____

BONUS FUN TIME!
Express *confess* with a drawing, or
invent a dictionary-style definition of your own.

steer

steer   •   [stIR]   •   \ 'stir \

- verb
1. *to direct the course of;*
2. *to set and hold to or pursue (a course)*

Can you hold the wheel and **steer** while I look at my phone for a bit?

SYNONYM

ANTONYM

WRITING TIME!
Use *steer* in an original sentence of your own creation.

_____

_____

_____

BONUS FUN TIME!
Express *steer* with a drawing, or
invent a dictionary-style definition of your own.

fierce

fierce   •   [fIRs]   •   \ ˈfirs \

- adjective
   1. marked by grim, pugnacious, or wild hostility;
   2. marked by furious unrestrained zeal or vehemence

Our neighbor's parakeet is really **fierce**, and I am afraid of it!

SYNONYM

ANTONYM

WRITING TIME!
Use *fierce* in an original sentence of your own creation.

_____

_____

_____

BONUS FUN TIME!
Express *fierce* with a drawing, or
invent a dictionary-style definition of your own.

arctic

arc·tic • [AHRk-tik] • \ ˈärk-tik \

---

adjective
1. bitterly cold;
2. in, characteristic of, or used in the region around the north pole

The **arctic** wind blew directly at us, making our noses really cold!

SYNONYM

ANTONYM

WRITING TIME!
Use *arctic* in an original sentence of your own creation.

_____

_____

_____

BONUS FUN TIME!
Express *arctic* with a drawing, or
invent a dictionary-style definition of your own.

solution

so·lu·tion   •   [suh-lOO-shuhn]   •   \ sə-ˈl(y)ü-shən \

- noun

> 1. *the action or process of solving a puzzle or problem;*
> 2. *the correct answer to a puzzle or problem*

Sal will always find a **solution** no matter how difficult the problem is.

SYNONYM

ANTONYM

WRITING TIME!

Use *solution* in an original sentence of your own creation.

BONUS FUN TIME!

Express *solution* with a drawing, or
invent a dictionary-style definition of your own.

SECTION FOUR: WORD REVIEW

Congratulations on learning ten amazing new words! Remember that the whole point of learning new vocabulary is actually to use it, so let's put your new vocabulary to use.

1. Review the words you've learned. Consider what ideas come to mind when you say the words. How about when you read the definitions?
2. Circle at least **two** of your favorites. You'll get to use these when you write your very own story!

journey ——— noun
1. *travel or passage from one place to another;*
2. *a long and often difficult process of personal development*

explore ——— verb
1. *to search through or into;*
2. *to make a first or preliminary study of*

gradual ——— adjective
1. *proceeding by steps or degrees : advancing step by step*

elegant ——— adjective
1. *tastefully correct and refined;*
2. *of a high grade or quality*

cause ——— noun
1. *a person, thing, fact, or condition that brings about an effect*

confess ——— verb
1. *to admit as true;*
2. *to acknowledge, especially after a previous denial*

steer ——— verb
1. *to direct the course of;*
2. *to set and hold to or pursue (a course)*

fierce ——— adjective
1. *marked by grim, pugnacious, or wild hostility;*
2. *marked by furious unrestrained zeal or vehemence*

arctic ——— adjective
1. *bitterly cold;*
2. *in, characteristic of, or used in the region around the north pole*

solution ——— noun
1. *the action or process of solving a puzzle or problem;*
2. *the correct answer to a puzzle or problem*

STORY FOUR

1. List the words you've chosen:

_____

2. Write a story that incorporates all of your chosen words. If you can't think of anything to write about, consider these suggestions:
   - Write a story involving time travel.
   - Write a story that takes place during your dream vacation.

Title: _____

_____

_____

_____

_____

_____

_____

_____

Wonderful Words for Third Grade Vocabulary & Writing Workbook ©2021 Grammaropolis LLC

Caption: _____

_____

_____

_____

_____

_____

_____

_____

_____

SECTION FIVE: WORD PREVIEW
Welcome to your ten new favorite words!

When you encounter a new word, take a moment to consider what it might mean.

1. Think about the word and circle what part of speech you think it is. *(Many words can act as more than one part of speech, depending on how they're used in the sentence, **so only choose one part of speech below**.)*

2. Come up with a brief definition of the word in the part of speech you've chosen. It doesn't have to be the *correct* definition—just do your best.

tentacle
Part of Speech: noun   verb   adjective

Definition:_____

_____

dangle
Part of Speech: noun   verb   adjective

Definition:_____

_____

scatter
Part of Speech: noun   verb   adjective

Definition:_____

_____

ability
Part of Speech: noun   verb   adjective

Definition:_____

_____

triumph
Part of Speech: noun   verb   adjective

Definition:_____

_____

mystify
Part of Speech: noun   verb   adjective

Definition:_____

_____

assist
Part of Speech: noun   verb   adjective

Definition:_____

_____

brilliant
Part of Speech: noun   verb   adjective

Definition:_____

_____

predict
Part of Speech: noun   verb   adjective

Definition:_____

_____

flexible
Part of Speech: noun   verb   adjective

Definition:_____

_____

tentacle

ten·ta·cle • [tEn-ti-kuhl] • \ ˈtentəkəl \

- noun

    1. a slender, flexible limb or appendage in an animal, used for grasping or moving about, or bearing sense organs

Did you know that an octopus can regrow a lost **tentacle**?

SYNONYM

ANTONYM

WRITING TIME!
Use *tentacle* in an original sentence of your own creation.

BONUS FUN TIME!
Express *tentacle* with a drawing, or
invent a dictionary-style definition of your own.

dangle

dan·gle   •   [dAnggUHl]   •   \ ˈdaŋ-gəl \

> **- verb**
>
> *1. to hang loosely especially with a swinging motion*
>
> Sarah and Fiona sat at the edge of the pool and **dangled** their feet over the water.

SYNONYM

ANTONYM

WRITING TIME!
Use *dangle* in an original sentence of your own creation.

_____

_____

_____

BONUS FUN TIME!
Express *dangle* with a drawing, or
invent a dictionary-style definition of your own.

scatter

scat·ter • [skAt-uhr] • \ ˈska-tər \

- verb
1. *to cause to separate into various widely removed parts;*
2. *to spread widely and at random by or as if by throwing*

When you blow on a dandelion, the seeds will **scatter** into the wind!

SYNONYM

ANTONYM

WRITING TIME!
Use *scatter* in an original sentence of your own creation.

BONUS FUN TIME!
Express *scatter* with a drawing, or
invent a dictionary-style definition of your own.

ability

abil·i·ty • [uh-bIl-uh-tee] • \ ə-ˈbi-lə-tē \

- noun
1. the quality or state of being able;
2. natural talent or acquired proficiency

Annie has a natural **ability** to draw, but I really have to work at it.

SYNONYM

ANTONYM

WRITING TIME!
Use *ability* in an original sentence of your own creation.

_____

_____

_____

BONUS FUN TIME!
Express *ability* with a drawing, or
invent a dictionary-style definition of your own.

triumph

tri·umph   •   [trIE-uhmf]   •   \ ˈtrī-əm(p)f \

- noun

   1. an occasion of victory especially such as to elicit satisfaction, exultation, or acclaim

We had ice cream to celebrate our **triumph** in the debate contest.

SYNONYM

ANTONYM

WRITING TIME!
Use *triumph* in an original sentence of your own creation.

BONUS FUN TIME!
Express *triumph* with a drawing, or
invent a dictionary-style definition of your own.

mystify

mys·ti·fy   •   [mIs-tuh-fie]   •   \ ˈmistə͵fī \

- verb
1. *to intentionally bewilder or perplex;*
2. *to involve in mystery*

Quinn's odd explanation for missing class **mystified** his teacher.

SYNONYM

ANTONYM

WRITING TIME!
Use *mystify* in an original sentence of your own creation.

BONUS FUN TIME!
Express *mystify* with a drawing, or
invent a dictionary-style definition of your own.

assist

as·sist   •   [uh-sIst]   •   \ ə-ˈsist \

> **- verb**
>> *1. to give support or aid*
>
> That nice young lady **assisted** the older gentleman across the street.

SYNONYM   ## ANTONYM

WRITING TIME!
Use *assist* in an original sentence of your own creation.

_____

_____

_____

BONUS FUN TIME!
Express *assist* with a drawing, or
invent a dictionary-style definition of your own.

brilliant

bril·liant • [brIl-yuhnt] • \ ˈbril-yənt \

- adjective
1. *sparkling with luster : very bright;*
2. *exceptionally clever or talented*

The **brilliant** sun reflected off the window and nearly blinded me.

SYNONYM

ANTONYM

WRITING TIME!
Use *brilliant* in an original sentence of your own creation.

_____

_____

_____

BONUS FUN TIME!
Express *brilliant* with a drawing, or
invent a dictionary-style definition of your own.

predict

pre·dict   •   [pri-dIkt]   •   \ pri-ˈdikt \

- verb

1. to declare in advance : prophesy

I **predict** that we will all get good grades on the test if we study hard!

SYNONYM

ANTONYM

WRITING TIME!
Use *predict* in an original sentence of your own creation.

BONUS FUN TIME!
Express *predict* with a drawing, or
invent a dictionary-style definition of your own.

flexible

flex·i·ble • [flEk-suh-buhl] • \ ˈflek-sə-bəl \

- adjective
  1. capable of being turned, bowed, or twisted without breaking;
  2. willing or ready to yield to the influence of others

Vinny's **flexible** plastic fork didn't break no matter how hard he tried.

SYNONYM

ANTONYM

WRITING TIME!
Use *flexible* in an original sentence of your own creation.

BONUS FUN TIME!
Express *flexible* with a drawing, or
invent a dictionary-style definition of your own.

Section Five: Word Review

Congratulations on learning ten amazing new words! Remember that the whole point of learning new vocabulary is actually to use it, so let's put your new vocabulary to use.

1. Review the words you've learned. Consider what ideas come to mind when you say the words. How about when you read the definitions?
2. Circle at least **two** of your favorites. You'll get to use these when you write your very own story!

tentacle —————— noun
1. *a slender, flexible limb or appendage in an animal, used for grasping or moving about, or bearing sense organs*

dangle —————— verb
1. *to hang loosely especially with a swinging motion*

scatter —————— verb
1. *to cause to separate into various widely removed parts;*
2. *to spread widely and at random by or as if by throwing*

ability —————— noun
1. *the quality or state of being able;*
2. *natural talent or acquired proficiency*

triumph —————— noun
1. *an occasion of victory especially such as to elicit satisfaction, exultation, or acclaim*

mystify —————— verb
1. *to intentionally bewilder or perplex;*
2. *to involve in mystery*

assist —————— verb
1. *to give support or aid*

brilliant —————— adjective
1. *sparkling with luster : very bright;*
2. *exceptionally clever or talented*

predict —————— verb
1. *to declare in advance : prophesy*

flexible —————— adjective
1. *capable of being turned, bowed, or twisted without breaking;*
2. *willing or ready to yield to the influence of others*

STORY FIVE

1. List the words you've chosen:

_____

2. Write a story that incorporates all of your chosen words. If you can't think of anything to write about, consider these suggestions:
   - **Write a story about the time when you met your best friend.**
   - **Write a story that takes place on a pirate ship.**

Title: _____

_____

_____

_____

_____

_____

_____

_____

Wonderful Words for Third Grade Vocabulary & Writing Workbook ©2021 Grammaropolis LLC

Caption: _____

_____

_____

_____

_____

_____

_____

_____

_____

_____

Wonderful Words for Third Grade Vocabulary & Writing Workbook ©2021 Grammaropolis LLC

SECTION SIX: WORD PREVIEW
Welcome to your ten new favorite words!

When you encounter a new word, take a moment to consider what it might mean.

1. Think about the word and circle what part of speech you think it is. *(Many words can act as more than one part of speech, depending on how they're used in the sentence, **so only choose one part of speech below**.)*

2. Come up with a brief definition of the word in the part of speech you've chosen. It doesn't have to be the *correct* definition—just do your best.

examine
Part of Speech: noun   verb   adjective

Definition:_____

_____

pastime
Part of Speech: noun   verb   adjective

Definition:_____

_____

crumple
Part of Speech: noun   verb   adjective

Definition:_____

_____

device
Part of Speech: noun   verb   adjective

Definition:_____

_____

deed
Part of Speech: noun   verb   adjective

Definition:_____

_____

opponent
Part of Speech: noun   verb   adjective

Definition:_____

_____

actual
Part of Speech: noun   verb   adjective

Definition:_____

_____

effect
Part of Speech: noun   verb   adjective

Definition:_____

_____

volunteer
Part of Speech: noun   verb   adjective

Definition:_____

_____

sensitive
Part of Speech: noun   verb   adjective

Definition:_____

_____

examine

ex·am·ine   •   [ig-zAm-uhn]   •   \ ig'zamən \

- verb

1. to test by an appropriate method;
2. to seek to ascertain : attempt to determine

At my last visit, the doctor **examined** my ears and heartbeat.

SYNONYM

ANTONYM

WRITING TIME!
Use *examine* in an original sentence of your own creation.

_____

_____

_____

BONUS FUN TIME!
Express *examine* with a drawing, or
invent a dictionary-style definition of your own.

pastime

pas·time   •   [pAs-tiem]   •   \ ˈpas-ˌtīm \

- noun

1. a specific form of amusement (as a game, hobby, or sport)

Birdwatching is my granny's favorite **pastime**, but I prefer yodeling.

SYNONYM

ANTONYM

WRITING TIME!
Use *pastime* in an original sentence of your own creation.

_____

_____

_____

BONUS FUN TIME!
Express *pastime* with a drawing, or
invent a dictionary-style definition of your own.

crumple

crum·ple   •   [krUHm-puhl]   •   \ ˈkrəm-pəl \

- verb
> 1. *to press or twist into folds or wrinkles;*
> 2. *to cause to collapse : break the resistance of*

I **crumpled** the wrapper into a ball before I threw it away.

SYNONYM

ANTONYM

WRITING TIME!
Use *crumple* in an original sentence of your own creation.

_____

_____

_____

BONUS FUN TIME!
Express *crumple* with a drawing, or
invent a dictionary-style definition of your own.

device

de·vice   •   [di-vIEs]   •   \ dә'vīs \

- noun
1. a thing made or adapted for a particular purpose, especially a piece of mechanical or electronic equipment

What is the purpose of that large electrical **device** you're carrying?

SYNONYM

ANTONYM

WRITING TIME!
Use *device* in an original sentence of your own creation.

BONUS FUN TIME!
Express *device* with a drawing, or
invent a dictionary-style definition of your own.

deed

deed   •   [dEEd]   •   \ ˈdēd \

- noun
    1. an action that is performed intentionally or consciously;
    2. a legal document, especially regarding property ownership

We needed someone to clean the bathroom, so I did the **deed**.

SYNONYM

ANTONYM

WRITING TIME!
Use *deed* in an original sentence of your own creation.

_____

_____

_____

BONUS FUN TIME!
Express *deed* with a drawing, or
invent a dictionary-style definition of your own.

opponent

op·po·nent • [uh-pOH-nuhnt] • \ ə-ˈpō-nənt \

> **- noun**
>
> *1. someone who competes against or fights another in a contest, game, or argument : a rival or adversary*
>
> It's always a good idea to salute your **opponent** after a match.

SYNONYM

ANTONYM

WRITING TIME!
Use *opponent* in an original sentence of your own creation.

BONUS FUN TIME!
Express *opponent* with a drawing, or
invent a dictionary-style definition of your own.

actual

ac·tu·al • [Ak-chuh-wuhl] • \ ˈak-chə(-wə)l \

- adjective
1. existing in fact;
2. in existence or taking place at the time

Is that an **actual** solution, or is it just wishful thinking?

SYNONYM

ANTONYM

WRITING TIME!
Use *actual* in an original sentence of your own creation.

BONUS FUN TIME!
Express *actual* with a drawing, or
invent a dictionary-style definition of your own.

effect

ef·fect　　　•　　　[i-fEkt]　　　•　　　\ i-ˈfekt \

> **- noun**
>
> *1. a change that occurs as a consequence of something that happens or is done*
>
> The **effect** of Jimmy's yelling in class was that we all got detention.

SYNONYM

ANTONYM

WRITING TIME!
Use *effect* in an original sentence of your own creation.

BONUS FUN TIME!
Express *effect* with a drawing, or
invent a dictionary-style definition of your own.

volunteer

vol·un·teer • [vahl-uhn-tIR] • \ ˌvälənˈtir \

- verb

1. to offer oneself for any service of one's own free will without solicitation or compulsion

I always **volunteer** to help fold the laundry because I love to fold!

SYNONYM

ANTONYM

WRITING TIME!

Use *volunteer* in an original sentence of your own creation.

BONUS FUN TIME!

Express *volunteer* with a drawing, or
invent a dictionary-style definition of your own.

sensitive

sen·si·tive • [sEn-suh-tiv] • \ ˈsen(t)-sə-tiv \

- adjective
>   1. *possessing a capacity for sensation or feeling;*
>   2. *easily and acutely affected*

I am most **sensitive** to tickling on the bottom of my right foot.

SYNONYM

ANTONYM

WRITING TIME!
Use *sensitive* in an original sentence of your own creation.

BONUS FUN TIME!
Express *sensitive* with a drawing, or
invent a dictionary-style definition of your own.

Section Six: Word Review

Congratulations on learning ten amazing new words! Remember that the whole point of learning new vocabulary is actually to use it, so let's put your new vocabulary to use.

1. Review the words you've learned. Consider what ideas come to mind when you say the words. How about when you read the definitions?
2. Circle at least **two** of your favorites. You'll get to use these when you write your very own story!

examine —— verb

1. to test by an appropriate method;
2. to seek to ascertain : attempt to determine

pastime —— noun

1. a specific form of amusement (as a game, hobby, or sport)

crumple —— verb

1. to press or twist into folds or wrinkles;
2. to cause to collapse : break the resistance of

device —— noun

1. a thing made or adapted for a particular purpose, especially a piece of mechanical or electronic equipment.

deed —— noun

1. an action that is performed intentionally or consciously;
2. a legal document, especially regarding property ownership

opponent —— noun

1. someone who competes against or fights another in a contest, game, or argument : a rival or adversary

actual —— adjective

1. existing in fact;
2. in existence or taking place at the time

effect —— noun

1. a change that occurs as a consequence of something that happens or is done

volunteer —— verb

1. to offer oneself for any service of one's own free will without solicitation or compulsion

sensitive —— adjective

1. possessing a capacity for sensation or feeling;
2. easily and acutely affected

STORY SIX

1. List the words you've chosen:

_____

2. Write a story that incorporates all of your chosen words. If you can't think of anything to write about, consider these suggestions:
   - Write a story in which you have an actual pet dinosaur.
   - Write a story that takes place after a natural disaster.

Title: _____

_____

_____

_____

_____

_____

_____

_____

Wonderful Words for Third Grade Vocabulary & Writing Workbook ©2021 Grammaropolis LLC

Caption: _____

_____

_____

_____

_____

_____

_____

_____

INDEX OF WORDS USED

CPSIA information can be obtained
at www.ICGtesting.com
Printed in the USA
JSHW020743290821
18255JS00002B/6